KEEP THEM HAPPILY PAYING YOU

4 Ways to Get Loyal Customers and Retain Them Via Social Media

Patrick Yafali

Keep Them Happily Paying You: 4 Ways to Get Loyal Customers and Retain Them Via Social Media

www.patrickyafalibooks.ca

ISBN: 978-1-77277-310-1

10-10-10 Publishing
Markham, ON
Canada

Printed in Canada and the United States of America

Table of Contents

How to Read this Book

Read the book more than once; and at the end of all chapters, use the space to make notes.

Acknowledgements

I would like to thank my mentor, Raymond Aaron, New York Times top ten bestselling author, for making it possible for me to write and publish this book, and for writing the foreword. I have also learned the best principles of goal setting, from Jack Canfield, another New York Times top ten bestselling author, with books like The Success Principles, and Chicken Soup for the Soul.

Thank you to my late mentor, Dr. Myles Munroe, New York Times top 10 bestselling author, with a library of bestselling books, like my favourite, *The Power of Character in Leadership: How Values, Morals, Ethics, and Principles Affect Leaders.* (He is the one who taught me leadership in the correct way.). Thank you to my spiritual mentors: Dr. Dayo Adeyemo, author of the book, *Walking in Your Prophetic Destiny;* and Dr. George Adegboye, author of many books, like *The Eagle Believer.* To my business mentor, Robert Kiyosaki, New York Times top ten bestselling author of *Rich Dad Poor Dad*; and Jack Canfield, New York Times top ten bestselling author, with *Chicken Soup for the Soul,* and *The*

Success Principles: How to Get from Where You Are to Where You Want to Be. Thank you to Les Brown, New York Times top 10 bestselling author of the book, *Live Your Dreams;* and Bob Proctor, international bestseller, with *You Were Born Rich.*

To my social media business mentors and teachers: Tai Lopez, who took social media by storm, and is co-founder of MentorBox, and founder of SMMA; Joe Soto, founder of Revenue Inbound; and Billy Gene, founder of Billy Gene is Marketing; and the many others who help and guide me through this journey.

To my lovely wife, Joanna: She is my lungs, my heart, and much more. To my parents and sibling, who always reminded me of my gift.

To my Lord and Saviour, Yeshua Hamashiach, who gave my life meaning.

Foreword

Does your business live up to is full potential? Can you visualize its growth?

In this world of fast technology, being sensible to change and adapting without losing your company's soul is a must.

Social media now is doing what the internet did many years ago, but many companies aren't catching the trend. If you can brand your company using social media, you can move it to another level.

In *Keep Them Happily Paying You*, you will learn what you need right away to create success for your company. Author Patrick Yafali will guide you and your employees on how to navigate the confusing world of social media marketing.

Read this book, and maximize the growth of your business!

Raymond Aaron
New York Times Bestselling Author

About the Author

Patrick Yafali has been at the forefront of the digital marketing sector for more than a decade. The award-winning author currently lives in Canada with his lovely wife, but he travels across the world, conducting seminars and workshops to help businesses build integrated, scalable, future proof, ROI-focused digital marketing strategies, and transform their businesses online.

Patrick has worked across multiple verticals, and has found the biggest gap, and that is strategic planning for any digital marketing campaign being overlooked across the board. He has worked for a Fortune 500 company, and much to his surprise, even the big players, in any vertical, have tunnel vision focus on just one part of digital marketing at all times. Now he has built his own company, First2Serve Marketing LTD., to help small and medium businesses grow, utilising social media marketing to generate leads that turn into loyal paying customers. He believes that small and medium businesses are the heart for economic growth in any part of the world.

With this book, he has shared his years of experience and in-depth blueprints that have helped many businesses across the world increase their bottom line profits online, and decrease their overall costs, all whilst keeping their digital marketing campaigns future proof and scalable.

Introduction

The remark I will give is that social media will never replace direct human interaction. It's just a tool to attract direct contact with the desired people. I remember when the tragedy of 9/11 happened. The stock market tanked, but the one that tanked the most was from airplane companies.

However, in the midst of this stock crisis, an investor was buying the stock at the lowest prices, and when he was interviewed about the reason he was buying those stocks, his response was, "As long as humans are humans, we will still want to have direct contact, like visiting our family members on the other side of the world."

Why I wrote this book:

Well, I wanted to shed light on the change that happened with this new world of social media, and the impact it had on businesses; especially small and medium ones, as they have a smaller amount of funds to use on traditional marketing, and many of them aren't as effective as they used to be.

I was tired of seeing the little guy struggling and getting crushed. Don't get me wrong; I do work with big enterprises also. However, my biggest clientele are the small and medium businesses, as in a city, you will have more small/medium businesses than bigger ones. A city needs both to grow, however; but many big businesses crush the small/medium one. I am talking about the young franchise that is competing with a giant such as McDonald's, or a family restaurant, open for years, competing with the Keg—and there are many more examples I could give. You get the picture!!

Now, why isn't traditional marketing appropriate for the small/medium business anymore? I will give you the major reason: The return on investment (ROI) is getting poorer and poorer. Let me give an example of what I mean by that. Imagine that you, a small/medium business, decide to use a giant billboard, for which you are paying $10,000 per month. They will charge this amount, for example, because 25,000 will see it in a month. Now, the issue is that yes, 25,000 will see it, but how many, in this busy world, will be able to stop to collect your info, and how many are your clients? And out of those who do get the info, how many call/text/email? The percentage is very low. The other problem is that many small/medium businesses have limited staff to receive those calls and follow up. This means that you lose another good portion of the rest of the people, which in many cases, is an ROI of less than 1%.

One of a business's strengths is a big list of current clients, and a list of new ones. Not working on a system that cultivates both, is the death of a business.

Now, imagine that you, the small/medium business, spend the same $10,000 to have 25,000 people a month see your ads, who are all potential clients. Let me give you an example to have a better picture: You have a pasta restaurant, and 25,000 pasta lovers see your ads (note that I did say, "pasta lover," and not just anybody). Because of your attractive ads, you will have 70% of them (17,500) respond to ads. Then, out of the 70%, 40% (7,000) will decide to come and give it a try. Now, let's say that they all eat your entry level pasta meals, at $7.50—this gives you $52,500 in new business, making a ROI of $42,500!!! Now, if they come in the 60-day period, it's still a ROI of $32,500!!

Now, let us not forget about the remaining 60% that didn't come. You will have a list of 10,500 new leads that you can re-market—wow!! These results happen all the time when you hire the right agency—like mine. We will handle all the processes of this system. Go to first2servemarketingltd.com to book a 30% off audit of your business.

This is the power of this new era of social media marketing. I would like this book to guide you in this new era so that you won't be the business that closes, but the one that is happily hiring new personnel to assist in your growth, decreasing the unemployment rate in your area— which is my LIFE GOAL, as well as serving your business with the correct strategy so that you may serve your services/goods to the many people yearning for it!

P.S. Social media is an ever-changing platform, like all things in the world. That's why our team keeps up to date with all the new updates, and bring them to you. By the end of this book, many updates have most likely happened, which is why, in any of our services, you will be served with the latest update.

Chapter 1

The Changes Made by the Internet in the 21st Century

I would like to comment a bit on the obvious: how the internet changed our world. The whole world has become smaller with the arrival of the internet. You can know in a flash what is happening in Australia, Japan, and in the Democratic Republic in the Congo, with a push of a button of your phone instead of your TV. You can experience travel through your cell phone, without taking a plane. And virtual technology will just make it more accessible.

That is my little take on what the internet has done to our world today.

I saw a funny movie, which gave me a good laugh: John English 2. As I had a good experience with the first one, I was eager to see the second instalment, and it didn't disappoint me. Well, I know some of you may not have liked it, but this isn't a book about movie critics. Therefore, to get back to my story, the movie was about stopping a villain, who they portrayed a little like an evil version of Mark Zuckerberg. The ultimate goal of the villain was to hold the world government hostage, by simply threatening to shut down the internet, and to get control through his scheme. Imagine all those super powers that were present, and had a noose around their neck simply because he now had the power to cut the internet!! Even though I had a good laugh, it still made me think a lot on how our way of life could have become miserable because of our dependence of the internet—from aviation control, work, security, and much more. This wasn't so, 50 years ago. Sorry for the scare—hope it wasn't too much.

Now, to talk a little about the impact on businesses. Well, we have more multimillion companies and millionaires today than ever before—simply because they are now SMALLER.

Let me give you 3 points on the subject of marketing, of which this book is focused on:

Traditional marketing: Traditional marketing is still alive. I believe that some of the traditional ways to get a client, such as door to door, referrals, and sometimes cold calling, still work as long as value is provided before anything else. However, the world is changing too fast, and the effectiveness of those ways is being reduced dramatically.

Internet marketing: This is where you use search engines, like Google, Bing, and Yahoo, to optimize your business—basically, to have people find you. This is also called a SEO. Here, you fight to rank in the top 5. The higher you rank, the better chance you have for people to come to your door.

Social media marketing: This one is the new wave, which will stay for a long time. Here, your flexibility is endless. This is the whole reason I wrote this book. I go into more detail in other chapters. But basically, it is when you utilise social media platforms, like Facebook, Instagram, Twitter, YouTube, and others, to attract people to your business.

Other examples of changes made by the internet, to business:

- I realised this change after I discovered the power of the internet, early in 2001. It eliminates the need of a physical store: EBay is one of the largest auction retailers, with a revenue of 8.97 billion dollars US (2016), by just allowing people and businesses to sell their goods. (It is free of charge for buyers to use the site, and sellers are charged a fee after they surpass their free listing.) Amazon is another company that is one of the largest retailers in the world, with a revenue of 135.98 billion dollars US, in 2016.
- It eliminates the need of physical products: Companies can now just send you a link to download a book (like the company, Kobo).

Others, like Oracle Corporation, which focuses on software, had a revenue of 37.73 billion dollars US, in 2017; not to mention social media companies, like Facebook, that had a revenue of 27.638 billion dollars US, in 2016. And Twitter, with a revenue of 2.53 billion dollars US, in 2016, and many more.

- It facilitates money transactions: Most of the banks now use e-Transfer, which allows any account holder to send money via the internet. Many countries, like US and Canada, use it.

My first experience with online business was in 2003, when me and couple of my friends founded Revolved.com. It was a company whose business model was like Kijiji, and this was before we even knew Kijiji existed. However, the high cost of building a website, and hosting, choked us before we could make a profit from it.

Notes

Notes

Chapter 2

Introduction of Branding for Small and Medium Businesses

This bonus chapter is one of my gifts to you. This subject is very dear to me as it is one that I spent many years learning, and am still learning, since I first read *Rich Dad Poor Dad,* by Robert Kiyosaki, in 2002. However, it was my mentor, Raymond Aaron, that made me love it, and he trained me in the mastery of it. This chapter will give a bit of understanding on the subject, as I will only give you some points throughout this book. Otherwise, it would be heavier than an Oxford dictionary. You can book an appointment with me, at this book bonus rate, for a 1-on-1 consultation on branding for your business or self-employment activity, on first2servemarketing ltd.com (look at the top of the home page).

A definition of a brand:

Simply put, it is a proper name that stands for a product or service. It stays in the consumer's mind, whether it's positive or negative. It is a personal perception of your company product or service.

My branding mentor, Raymond, who is doing the forward for this book, taught me that branding is basically a promise you make—a promise that you keep. (For example, if you are always late, that's your brand.)

He taught me many things in my branding journey that I will share with you.

Branding makes you trustworthy and known:

Having a brand makes you and your business more special than others. A brand, such as Apple, speaks volumes, and many of its customers also swear by it.

In my years of studying branding, I discovered that branding also gives potential clients/customers a feeling or comfort level that they associate with you. The stronger and more positive that feeling is, the more easily and more frequently they will want to do business with you. That's what I also confirmed with my mentor.

Branding differentiates you from others. When you do it correctly, you make yourself better than the competition, and you make yourself more memorable and unforgettable. The interesting part is that even if your service/product is the same as every other product like it, branding makes you and your service/product the first product a consumer thinks about when thinking about making a decision to purchase.

Branding pre-sells your product:

We are in the era where people are trying to do everything quickly: microwavable foods, drive-throughs, etc. Therefore, we, as business owners, must be the first to grab their attention—in a split second. When someone is looking to go on a date, they should know your restaurant name, before having to google it. The stronger your brand, the less they google about it. For example, I don't need to google anymore to find the closest Apple store in my city—I know where they are!

The stronger the branding, the more people are likely to think in terms of your products, rather than product category. This is something my mentor taught me.

The branding ladder:

The branding ladder is a sort of unity of measurement for you and your business. The higher you climb, the more influential you become. This ladder is different from others; you can't skip the steps but can only get there one step at a time. The ladder has 5 definite steps: brand absence, brand awareness, brand preference, brand insistence, and brand advocacy. I will give you a brief definition of them.

Brand absence: This is where many start up, and where many stay. This is where you have no brand whatsoever, except your own name. This is the most horrible place to be, no matter how good your services or products are. However, if there is a way to climb up, you can find it by booking your appointment at first2servemarketingltd.com, and claiming your bonus rate. I will give you an example for a better picture: John Doe names his company, John Doe Plumbers. I see it every day—lawyers, real estate agents, dentists—and they all make the same fatal mistake of almost always using their own names.

P.S. Don't get me wrong; you can make your name a brand, like the Hilton hotels, Wendy's, etc. However, to do so, you must brand it from the start. For example, Jane Doe the realtor becomes, "I am Jane Doe, the realtor who gets you into a home larger than you thought you could afford." This is how one of my mentors helped one of his clients.

Brand awareness:

When my mentor, Raymond, told me that 97% of businesses don't reach this level, I have to admit that

I was spooked. Being on this ladder will put you in the top 3% of your industry. You want people to be aware of you and your business. When person X speaks to person Y, and says, "Have you heard of 24/7 Plumber?" you want the answer to be, "Oh, yes!"

Now, when you are here, don't get too comfortable. Just because people know you, it doesn't necessarily mean that they want to buy. For example, I know of Acer, but I buy from Apple.

Brand preference:

Ladder 3 is definitely a real step up. This means that people prefer to buy from you rather than your competition.

They know for sure the difference between you and others, and you are their first choice.

Brand preference is clearly better than brand awareness, but it's less than half way up the branding ladder.

However, I will say it again: Don't get too comfortable here, as this isn't enough. Simple example: I have a business membership with Avis car rental. I went to a wedding in Edmonton, and at the airport, when I went to pick up my car that I had reserved over the phone, they told me that I couldn't, because of an error that happened in the past. In my head, I had one question: Why didn't the nice lady, whom I had spoken to on the phone, tell me? So, even though they were my preferred brand, I didn't spend my time trying to fix the situation. I just went to National, with whom I also have a business account. They lost my business that day because of it.

Brand insistence:

This is when you make it you, and only you—when your customers are so committed to your product or service that they won't accept a substitute. All companies strive to reach this level.

Brand insistence means that someone's experience with your product, in terms of performance, durability, customer service, and image, has been sufficiently exceptional. As a result, the product has earned an incredible level of loyalty. When you reach this level, your customers will literally not buy from someone else, even when you are not available. They would rather look for your products elsewhere. This is the best of the best. I will take myself as an example again. I know I'm giving them free publicity, but that's what brand insistence does.

Apple hardware is what I would use over Microsoft. I would pick the iPad Pro over the Surface anytime.

Brand advocacy:

This last ladder is the highest you can reach. This is when customers are so happy with your product that they want everyone in their circle of influence to know about it and use it. However, most companies can only aspire to get to this level of customer satisfaction. Apple and Samsung are two of those few large corporations that have brand advocates all over the world.

Brand advocacy will do 5 marvellous things:

- Provide a level of visibility that you couldn't pay for even if you tried
- Deliver free advertising and public relations
- Afford a level of credibility that literally can't be bought
- Provide pre-sold prospective customers/clients
- Increase profits exponentially

Moving Up The Branding Ladder

Most small and medium businesses get stuck on the first two ladders. However, you don't have to be stuck there. There is a way to move up.

By following some principals, you could be well on your way up, faster than you could imagine. For the purpose of not making this book an Oxford dictionary size, I will give you one system that I developed. (P.S. This works very well when used in combination with other systems. Book your branding consultation at this book bonus price, at first2servemarketing ltd.com.)

The WOW Effect

This is something that I found out after intensive studies and mentorship with Raymond. He gave it the name, WOW. It is the pleasantly unexpected–the extra mile that you and your business go. It is a great way to brand yourself and set yourself apart.

For every WOW you give a customer, you are on your way to having brand advocates. No matter how small the WOW is, it boosts your business growth. Keep in mind that people tell their family and friends about WOWs, via phone, social media, or even blogging. Look at it this way: For every WOW, your customer moves up the branding ladder. The WOW can't be just for show; it must relate to what your business does, and be meaningful to your customers.

An example of a common WOW is free delivery, and no payment for 3months. Now, a little warning:

If a customer gets a few non-WOWs (bad experiences), they become ex-customers, and they go from being a frequent buyer to an "only when I need it." Even worse, they will tell others about their horrible experience.

Let me tell you about a personal WOW that I received from the Kitchener Stars Men's Shop's manager, Christian Gaudette. I was traveling to Nigeria for my spiritual mentor's 60th birthday, in December.

Now, in Canada, December is winter time, which means that most stores didn't have suits appropriate for summer at that time.. As he could see how desperate I was, he helped find some linen suits that his employee hadn't been able to find for me. Plus, he gave me a complimentary pocket square. I am telling you, I was so relieved that he went the extra mile for me.

One of the ways that I operate my business, to give the best WOW, is to first select my ideal clients, and not take more than my team can handle. Then we give our undivided attention to them. Our motto is a tailor made experience just for you.

The PMW

This is years of studies on human behaviour and psychology, based on scientific proof. When I was going for interviews, my career coach used to tell me that first impressions matter, and that you need to dress up in business attire. I bet you heard that before. So, I will have to put on my business suit and tie for the occasion. It was later on that I understood that it's a principle that stays true for many other things, like your first date, prom night, awards ceremony, and much more. That's why the first letter of the acronym is P, for Physic.

P for Physic: Physic simply represents the outside look or the first image people will perceive through their very own eyes. That's why companies spend a lot of money on logos, packaging, and style. For example, the slick look of the iPhone has been copied by its competition, over and over again. In my company, black and gold is used as the theme color.

M for Mind: Commercials have one goal, and that is for you to keep the products or services in mind. Seminars, workshops, and more are all used to help keep you in the minds of your customers. This is a billion-dollar fight.

W for Will: This is where you earn your money. It's when the potential customer makes the decision to become a PAYING CUSTOMER. By utilising the P and M properly, you will be in the position to influence your customer to buy from you instead of your competition.

The PMW system is a unique system developed by my company, First2Serve Marketing LTD. We used universal principles that have been effective for the past thousands of years. It works for virtually any field (realtor firms, insurance companies, dentists, hotels, lawyers, and much more).

You are already on your journey of the branding ladder. Some of you are at the bottom, some are in the middle, and some are almost at the top. My team would be happy to provide our assistance with your journey. You may book your call with us to find out how we may assist you, and if we are a good fit for you and your brand. Feel free to visit first2serve marketingltd.com/patrickyafalibooks.ca.

In conclusion, this chapter is only an introduction of why branding is very important for small and medium businesses. Our branding package utilises a combined experience of 30+ years, between me and my mentor. I hope you enjoy this book. It is better that you take action today to be on your way to greatness. It would be my pleasure to assist you in this journey.

(P.S. Book your branding consultation at this book bonus price, at first2servemarketingltd.com.)

Notes

Notes

Chapter 3

Funnel

I like the funnel strategy a lot; it's like the word says. You will funnel people from the mass to get quality people that you want to do business with you, and vice versa. It is the place where you filter the curious from the serious.

My strategy is to also get quality leads to enter the funnel. This allows you to have a higher percentage of people that want to do business with you—the crème of the crème.

a. What is a funnel? A funnel is the system used to gather your leads from various sources, like Facebook ads, YouTube, Instagram, and others.
b. Purpose of a funnel: To keep it simple, it is just to filter the window shopper from the paying one, in a very effective manner.
c. Why must a funnel be created in advance? This will allow business owners to have a funnel that can be tested, to select a campaign winner.
d. The steps of the funnel: The steps are simple but must be set properly in order to work and give you real data: lead – prospect – paying customer.

Conclusion: A funnel must be tested for its effectiveness, and be adaptable for various industries. The people that will tell you that I have the perfect funnel, are liars, as the steps of the funnel don't change. The process of each step does change. For example, you can't market for women the same way you do for men, or for a 19-year-old the same way you do for a 40-year-old person. You need to be aware of this so that you don't waste your hard-earned cash on someone that will give you little results. Register for a free webinar, at first2serve marketingltd.com.

A heads up: The forgotten life blood of your funnel

Because of how many people that have started using a messenger platform, like Facebook messenger and others, many people, and many other agencies, think that email will become irrelevant. However, it is far from the truth, as more than 4.5 billion email accounts exist. Therefore, email is still relevant. The reason that email is still relevant is because it's like the digital version of a contacts book. This is where you collect info on your clients, or potential clients, to keep on adding value.

This is where you can give updates that are relevant for a specific client, do follow up, and add value with new knowledge, and even offer additional services. I learned many types of strategies to build an email list. The bigger your list, the bigger your future earning potential. You can book a 30-minute, free consultation to find out how to grow your business email list, at first2servemarketingltd.com.

Notes

Notes

Chapter 4

The 1st Way: YouTube

Why do business owners need a YouTube account?

The reason why businesses need a YouTube channel is so that they can be the first to reach you. 1,300,000,000+ accounts exist in the world, and close to 5 billion videos are viewed every MINUTE. Many of the internet gurus believe that videos will take over almost anything. My social media mentor, Tai Lopez, confirmed it.

Another mentor of mine, Sifu Dan Lok, wrote a book on another source of wealth, which is called Audience. His YouTube channel grew, in less than 4years, from 100K subscribers to more than 1.6 million. Few people can claim this. The most viewed video on YouTube so far is "Shape of You," by Ed Sheeran, with more than 4.07 billion views—imagine that. Let me make a point on the wealth of audience.

The wealth of audience:

Audience is the new wealth in business marketing, especially via YouTube, which is the best platform to promote. A little story: The worldwide famous singer, Justin Bieber, was able to get a record because he had a growing audience on YouTube. He is one of the top 10 people that have the most viewed video, one of them being the song, "Sorry," which has 3.08 billion plus views so far. Now, imagine that there are 7 billion plus people on our beautiful planet Earth, and he had 3.08 billion plus watch him. That's the leverage that YouTube brings for people and businesses.

YouTube influencer

Let me touch on the YouTube influencer. Of all the video platforms, I would say that YouTube is king. It's where many programs, like the masterclasses and many others do their publicity. The stronger your presence on YouTube, the higher your business can scale. Now, influencers are the ones with a larger amount of subscribers, with videos that are viewed by many.

The rule of video is to always, and I mean always, lead with value.

Now, how do you utilise YouTube for your business? Example for a dentist: You will need a channel that provides tips, and educates on the benefit of good dental hygiene, such as why we need to floss, how to correctly floss, the danger of not teaching children to floss, and much more. Another example is for hotels. Many times, I just see fewer than 20 videos, which are just too generic. Now, what you can do is have a staff member video the value of great housekeeping. This will show how much you care for the place that people will call a temporary home.

Therefore, you must, in this day and age, have an audience on YouTube, to take your business to the next level.

Bonus secret: You will rank higher on Google search when you have a video for your service, rather than just a blog or website. Our team can assist with this, as part of our services. Book your 30-minute, free consultation, at first2serve marketingltd.com

Now I will give you 5 points on the beauty of YouTube:

The YouTube channel: This is like what its name says—a channel. Basically, it is your own channel to market your service and products of your company. If, for example, you own hotels, you will need a channel that displays the perks of your establishment; like what people can expect from choosing your place for a wedding venue, a vacation, a celebration, and more. Now, the better the video, the more views and subscribers you will get, and the more people will know about your hotels.

Subscribers: On your channel, you will want people to become subscriber. They are the people that will most likely want to know about your services by viewing the videos you post; and they will tell their friends and family about it. They also give feedback, good and bad. This is why, at the end of all your videos, you must ask people to subscribe, as they will also become organic leads. Organic leads are the ones for which you don't need to do much paid advertising in order to get them.

Make viewers view more of your content: The proper use of your channel is to redirect the viewer to watch more of your product content. This works best when you arrange your playlist properly. For example, if you have a dental office, and you made a video tutorial on dental hygiene, you would like them to watch another video on the benefits of dental hygiene. What you will do, at the end of the video, is to let your audience know that they can watch more by clicking the play list. This will maximize your business promotion. The more viewers watch more content, the more efficient your channel becomes.

Become an authority: The success of your channel will establish you as an authority in your field. You become the first place people check when they are looking for an answer. For example, you are a real estate broker in your town. Now, when people want to buy, or sell their houses or properties, they will google a person if they weren't referred, and it is you that they will find. By viewing your video, they will make their choice, but because you have a more efficient channel, you will be the better choice, as you will stand out as an authority above your competition.

Value driven: Your channel should be driven by giving value to your audience, and not just by selling your service or products, or you will have less people wanting to be part of your channel. The more value you give, the more you will attract a quality audience who will be happy to become your loyal paying customer. For example, if you own a restaurant that serves healthy meals, instead of inviting people to come and eat at your place, make a lot of videos about the benefit of eating meals that are cooked with the freshest ingredients. The more you share those values, the more your business will touch your audience.

In conclusion, YouTube is growing, and is becoming more and more valuable for business. By booking your consultation with me, at first2serve marketingltd.com, we can explore the opportunity that your business can take advantage of.

Notes

Notes

Chapter 5

The 2nd Way: Facebook

Why do business owners need a Facebook account?

The reason business owners need a Facebook account is because of the 2,000,000,000+ users out of the 7.6 billion people in the whole world. All of those people are available to be marketed to, for your services or products. This is the potential reach that any business owner has in their grasps. The beauty of Facebook is that it is free, and for users to have an account, they can list their name, date of birth, occupation, and more. All this data is available to business owners.

#Facebook Pixel

Why would I recommend, to business owners, the use of Facebook Pixel? It's simply because this tool will help the business owner's marketing campaign to be more visible to potential clients/customers.

Facebook Pixel is one of the newest tools on Facebook, and it's used for retargeting interested clients/customers. This strategy will help you focus your marketing on interested people who visit your website. This will save you the trouble of chasing people that were never interested in you, and save on your marketing cost.

The benefit is that you are now able to remarket your services/products to people that have the highest chance of being converted to being customers/clients.

The way Facebook Pixel works is by creating a pixel from your business Facebook, and then setting up the code to your website and your Facebook page. This is a tracking system that will give you much data on your visitor, such as which page they view, how long they watch your videos for, and more. This is a great way to know more about them without them putting any personal info, like an email, in your website or Facebook ads. Then, just retarget them with your products, increasing their interest until they buy.

Retained clients via Facebook

This is an extra step that business owners should use in order to create a group of all paying customers/clients. It will allow you to update them on changed or new services, and others, in a private way. However, the best way to utilise your group would be to get feedback from your clients/customers in order to improve your business overall.

The Facebook group has 3 settings of privacy:

1. Open means that both the group and its members, and their comments, are visible to the public (which includes non-members), but they cannot interact without joining.

2. Closed means the group and its members are visible to the public, but their comments are not visible until the user has joined the group.

3. Secret means that nothing can be viewed by the public unless a member specifically invites another user to join the group.

Out of the 3 settings, the last 2 will give your clients/customers a more exclusive feeling. And you can add to this exclusivity by letting them know that they will be the first to know about new services, discounts, etc.

Tips: The senior clients/customers also help the newest ones, which saves you time on customer service.

P.S. Things are always changing, and our company keeps up with the changes.

For your additional bonus, visit: keepthem happilypaying.com

Notes

Notes

Chapter 6

The 3rd Way: Instagram

Why do business owners need an Instagram account?

The reason why Instagram made the list is simply because of its 800 million users (in 2017). One of the interesting aspects of Instagram is that it was bought by Facebook. They also created a feature that allowed Facebook content (photos) to be linked to Instagram, which is making a lot of Facebook users open Instagram accounts. This will then increase the visibility of your business. The more visible you are, the more leads you will have access to, to potentially change them into paying clients/customers.

Now, the question is, how should a business owner use their Instagram account? Well, there are many ways for them to use it, which would make this book like a dictionary. However, I will give some of most strategic ways.

As a catalogue: Instagram was first created as an online photo album for the user, where they could share photos of their daily life.

The way the business owner should use this feature is to display products or services. The picture should be of high quality. For example, if you own a restaurant, you should display pictures of the menu, which can make someone hungry just by looking at it. Some pictures could include the waiter serving an eager customer. The picture should push someone to call and make a reservation. Include the description of the display plate. If you are in the fashion industry, for example, a picture of suits should show the quality of the material used to make the suits. You can create a slide show that shows the making of the suits. Creativity here is a must.

Tips: Always have a call to action in all pictures/contents, for people to go on your profile bio link. Neglecting to have a CTA (call to action) is equal to losing thousands of daily leads, who will never become your clients; thus, having an unproductive and unreliable Instagram platform.

As coupons: As Instagram works well with pictures, offering your services or products discount can be used with it. This will make your clients eager to check your Instagram, and you also save tree!!

Instagram is a platform that works well for daily info of the latest discount for the general public. For example, you own a dental office, and you would like to get more clients. So, you create a discount for teeth whitening, for which you will create coupons showing a beautiful smile, including some details. For your potential clients to redeem it, they will need to book an appointment, which will require them to enter their email and phone number. This will help you generate lots of leads, where even if someone cancels their appointment, you will have their contact follow-up information, and will be able to offer additional services. Thus, you never lost the leads.

Social proof: This one will help boost your credibility and also encourage others to check your business. We all know the power of testimonies. They never go out of style, as they are one of the most powerful marketing methods used by any business. And that is why they should be part of your Instagram.

This can be done by a happy client's/customer's photos, with their own comments on the experience or event, with a short video of them expressing the value your services or products help them with For example, you are a chiropractor, and you assisted one of your clients, who is satisfied. You will just ask him/her to make a 1-minute video of how satisfied they are, or a picture with their comment. But to add to the power, ask them if they have their own Instagram on which to post it.

Launching your Instagram account the right way

For this portion, I will touch on one of the major tips on setting up your Instagram account, as this platform has its own way to be utilised for your business growth.

The growth is linked to the attraction formula, which includes daily posts (3–8 per day). People come to Instagram for a daily dose; it's also where they will observe you/your business. For example, a restaurant will post a picture that describes a customer's experience with one of their menu items; or the great effects of their gluten-free menu: the body can enjoy it without harm.

One aspect of the daily posting is to never miss a day, especially for new or renewed launches. Diligence is lord here, and consistency is a must. This is to create the snowball effect.

What must be avoided is content that is not relevant to the target market. It should always be valuable and relevant to them; otherwise, it will be hard for them to relate (e.g., a restaurant just posting about the weather).

The picture quality on Instagram must be good, as aesthetics is king there. One of my mentor's businesses generated 20 million in sales, just from getting leads from the posting quality.

The bio link:

The most important real estate in your Instagram account is your bio. This is the place where you will need to put the link for your funnels. In that link, you must have a compelling offer for your clients/ customers, which will require them to enter their info to receive it. From there, you have your leads that you will be able to follow up on. Always follow the rule of offering something of value to them. Very important: Your bio real estate shouldn't be used for your website link, as they are not yet ready to buy. I saw a lot of people doing it the wrong way, and they have created a situation where you lose many leads. Let me give you a simple example, using a physio-therapist: Your bio link should include an eBook offer about 5 problems that physiotherapy solves. With this, you will get qualified leads who either need your services or know someone that does. The goal is to take them to the environment of your control, where the rules of Instagram stop and yours begin. This is a serious, fundamental aspect of your bio real estate. When you are in control, you have to create the flow that will create the interaction with your potential buyer. Therefore, all you need is the correct funnel (I will touch more on funnels, down the road) to transform your leads. In some cases, they will just reach out to you themselves, after reading the value received. This sets you apart from the competition that just wants the sale, and are pushy about it.

The Famous Hashtag:

Instagram is famous for its postings using the hashtag function. It's so famous that some people will say it in their verbal and texting conversation.

Every post needs a hashtag that is relevant to it, as this is the Instagram language that people will relate to.

There is a special bonus on how to find more leads, at keepthempaying.com.

Retaining clients via Instagram

This section is about what follows after you are successful at getting customers. Now, just to touch a bit on an important part: Instagram is a channel that you will like to use primarily to collect emails, and not to make a sale. The formula that you want to use is: leads - prospects - customers. In that formula, Instagram will get you the leads for your sales funnels, but not the sales themselves.

Tips: Your website for the funnel must be mobile optimized, as more than 90% of people using Instagram are on mobile.

The customer retention portion for Instagram can be used to have your existing clients receive an additional discount, or other value items, by sharing an experience through their Instagram pages. This will create the platform to make them repeating customers, and also create free advertising for you (also called organic leads). You will have friends and family members, of your clients, wanting to use your service because of a testimony. I do offer an additional bonus through keepthemhappily paying.com.

Bonus lead secret (for website only)

You have to engage with your competitor and influencer page, and be present on their page by commenting on their post and liking it. This will drive some people to you (the organic market). However, this must be done vice versa; and always write back to your community, and treat them like a pink diamond.

I just need to stress again that your Instagram isn't a selling platform but a lead generation one. Always lead with value for people to follow. Also, your number one asset is your bio link, which I can't stress enough, and I really want to make sure that all businesses use it. You can receive my help to set it up, as part of my consultation package, and you can submit an application of qualification via keepthemhappilypaying.com.

Here are 3 examples of things you can post to attract leads:

1. Podcast audio that delivers value on the problems your business solves (with a call to action)
2. Blog/eBook that addresses 2–3 major concerns of your client base (with call to action)
3. Coupons for services or products (with a call to action)

P.S. I do offer, included in my consulting package, the setup of those options, at keepthemhappily paying.com.

Notes

Notes

Chapter 7

The 4th Way: Twitter

Let talk about Twitter, the little blue birdie. I used to dislike it, as the notices would fill up my phone, and the noise was annoying. But I hadn't understood its true value. First, it has 335 million users worldwide, and it's growing. Second, it ranks well in organic search results when someone googles your business name. And third, it's a loud place where you can post at least 8 times per day to strengthen your brand. However, it's not for customer gain but mostly for client retention.

I will give you the 2 best ways to utilise your Twitter account, which should be the basis of why you need that account. By using it that way, may be the only way for many businesses.

Best way to use Twitter: The most basic way to utilize your Twitter account is by announcements. Blast as many of them as possible to have your potential or existing clients know firsthand what value you would like to share.

For attracting new clients, I will use the example of a local food restaurant. You can blast a message about a new location that you are opening, and that the first 10 people to make a reservation will have the chance to get an expensive bottle of wine, complimentary. Then you will just update the process of the people that are reserving all day long, until you have a winner. You will state that the winner will be revealed by email, which will push people to sign up for your email list. (Remember, your email list is your business blood.)

For listening/feedback: This is a skill that is used less and less, as people will just talk about themselves, their offer, their deals, etc. However, listening to people will give you great insight for improvement, for FREE. This makes the clients feel valued. For example, to retain existing clients, you can ask them what they want to see improved, kept, or changed. This is vital for business growth. McDonald's used to only serve burgers and fries, but now they have kids' meals, toys, coffee, salads, and much more. The difference is that McDonald's paid to get surveys done, but you don't have to.

I know it's hard to get criticism and complaints, but it's worse to see how people want to change your baby (business). However, remember why you are in business in the first place. Most of us want to provide improvements for people or businesses, by offering our products or services. The car you drive has changed over the years; the houses built today have changed—basically, everything changes—but the core always stays the same: A house will still be a shelter first, and cars will always be vehicles to get from A to B. So, don't be afraid (I was also afraid); I will assist you, step by step.

Notes

Notes

Chapter 8

Copywriting

This is a bonus chapter to help in understanding the behind-the-scenes action that helps make the best ads for your businesses. This chapter is something that I have learned from my copywriting mentor, Raymond Duke.

The first rule of copywriting is that it's not about your business but about the readers. People care most about what interests them—their care, their beliefs, their dislikes. Let me share 4 tips with you that you can use today.

Use verbs:

When writing a post about a special offer, use active verbs: get (this discount); click (the link below); download (our restaurant menu). This type of verb will trigger in the brain a will to action.

Keep it simple:

Do not use complicated words that most people don't use in their daily language. Also, when writing for an offer, try to keep it to 1 or 2 syllables.

Use questions that call out your market:

By using certain types of questions, it will help attract your potential clients to read. Let them know that you are talking to them.

For example, you own a hair salon (using a picture to give the reader an idea). Would you trust this woman with your hair?

Be specific:

For this one, you have to avoid being vague, and not leave things for interpretation. The use of numbers and names works well.

For example, you own a restaurant, and in your ads, you don't want your address to be missed. We (business name) are right out on Highway 7; head east for 7 minutes. We are by the red building, "John Doe." Don't forget to ask for Julie, for your 50% discount.

Use this tip in your company, and watch the change and increased engagement by your clients, which will lead to a revenue increase. And if you want our team to help, we will gladly assist you. Just book a call at www.first2servemarketingltd.com or www.patrickyafalibooks.ca.

How to get social media fans and existing customers to write copy for you:

Most business owners and entrepreneurs who have been active in their field for 5 years plus, already have fans and existing customers. Now, this is a gold mine for feedback and additional revenue, with less marketing expenses.

As the title of the book says, keep them happily paying you. This section will give you a guideline on how to provide better service to your client base, on what they want you to give.

This is a 3-part process that I learned from one of my mentors.

Identify what they want:

Check your fans' interests in your business service areas by checking who they follow other than you; check what they said on yelp. For example, you own a pastry shop that has pies as a signature item. You would just need to check what they said about pies.

Give them what they want:

The next step is to give them what they want by writing an e-Book (using Facebook ads) on pies, based on what they talk about the most. For example, 3 toppings that will make your pie-eating experience mouth-watering. Add a discount coupon code for them to come taste those pies with the 3 toppings.

Pay attention to feedback:

The last step is to get more feedback in order to better the experience. Just ask them to give a testimonial, on your Facebook, Twitter, and Instagram accounts. Use that to create more value- based content. Remember to pay attention to the negative comments, in order to improve. However, keep in mind that others will just badmouth you.

This strategy will skyrocket your social media presence, which will scale your business to a much higher plane. This has worked for all types of clients.

Notes

Notes

Chapter 9

The FSAR System

In this chapter, I will touch briefly on our unique system, which was developed for the sole purpose of producing the desired result for you.

The acronym, FSAR, stands for what our company believes and stands for. Therefore, the meaning of the FSAR system is F(irst), S(erve), A(cquisition), R(etention) System. In previous chapters, you will have seen that I gave many examples of what processes to follow when doing your social media marketing. In most of them, you will see that I always want us to focus on giving value first. Now, let us break down the system.

F for First

Always, and I mean always, think what the first thing(s) is that you can offer to your clients to give them a taste of what you can do for them. For example, when I go to the mall, I will almost always have someone that will ask me to taste or try their service/product sample. This is a universal law. It doesn't always have to be something complimentary.

You have to think of something that will give your clients value, but with a lower risk or cost to you. It can be done before or after, depending on your service/product.

Therefore, always think about what value you can offer first. This book is a prime example of me following the system.

S for Serve

This part deals with the delivery method you choose to give your service/product, whether it is the sample or the actual product. In my case, for the sample, I use this book as the delivery method, but I also use seminars/webinars, workshops, etc. I use social media to promote my delivery method. This can be adapted in all industries.

The goal is always to give the picture of the value your clients will get in choosing you.

A for Acquisition

The acquisition is the vehicle that we will use to acquire the new clients. This process is decided in the consultation we do with you. After evaluation, we will find out which social media platform to focus on first.

Once we know the vehicle, we can now work on the type of ads. Those will be determined based on your target market. For example, you own a hotel, and you want to acquire families for a vacation package. In this case, we will target only parents and not the children. All ads will focus on being appealing to parents.

R for Retention

The last part is designed keep them paying you, as the title of the book states. Many businesses are very weak in this area, and this includes larger ones as well. Businesses usually only focus on spending a lot to get new clients, but are poor at creating new revenue from existing clients. The common way to retain clients is through customer service.

However, the best way is to keep on adding value for your clients, on top of the customer service. For example, a dentist most likely has the date of birth of all his clients in his files. You can retarget your existing clients, on their birthdays, for teeth whitening that they didn't yet receive during the year. This, combined with the WOW factor (check branding chapter), will create explosive growth in your business.

Notes

Notes

Conclusion

I hope you have enjoyed reading this book as much as I enjoyed writing it for you. This knowledge will give you a tremendous advantage on the market. Read the book again and again, and share it with your marketing team.

However, would you like my team to assist you in this journey of social media marketing so that you can focus on what you do best, instead of using your valuable time to learn this progress yourself, perhaps being unsatisfied with the result you are getting? You can book a call with us at patrickyafalibooks.ca. It would be a pleasure for us to assist you.

As I am also a firm believer of sharing our blessings with the less fortunate, every year, I will donate 30% of the book sales revenue to a chosen charitable organisation. You can partake in offering your choice by submitting the name of your charity to be part of a draw.

P.S. All charities must assist people in these categories: homeless, orphans, and widows.

Notes

Notes

Bonuses

Access these bonuses (included with the book) at patrickyafalibooks.ca.

- 30-minute complimentary consultation
- 20% of full social media marketing consultation
- 1-month complimentary social media management (with the purchase of the consultation package at full price)
- 20% off branding package

www.ingramcontent.com/pod-product-compliance
Lightning Source LLC
Chambersburg PA
CBHW070844070326
40690CB00009B/1685

* 9 7 8 1 7 7 2 7 7 3 1 0 1 *